SONS & SHADOWS

By AXEL JORDAN

SONS & SHADOWS

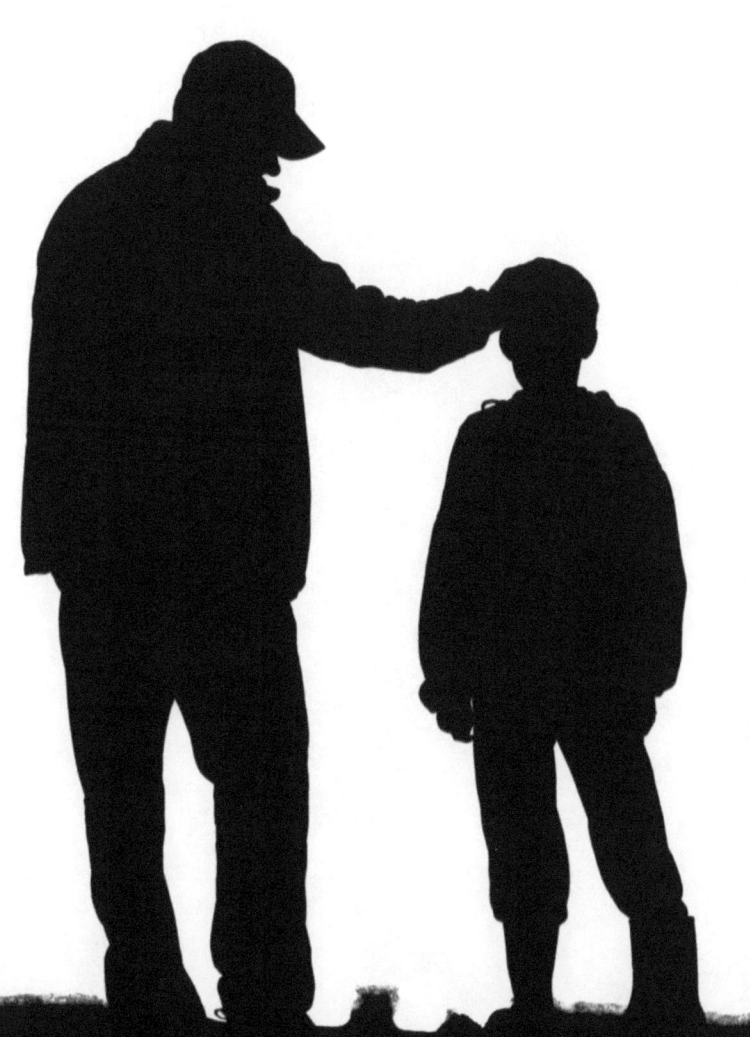

DEDICATION

For the sons seeking understanding, the fathers striving to heal, and everyone daring to break cycles of pain.

Dedicated to the strength it takes to forgive, the courage to grow, and the love that binds us, even in imperfection.

Trigger Warning

This book contains discussions and personal reflections on topics that may be triggering or distressing to some readers. Sensitive themes explored within these pages include:

- **Emotional Abuse and Trauma:** Reflections on strained father-son relationships and the lasting impact of emotional neglect.
- **Substance Abuse and Addiction:** Personal accounts of struggles with addiction, including the numbing effects of drugs and alcohol as coping mechanisms.
- **Sexual Assault:** Mentions of past traumatic experiences that may involve references to sexual violence and exploitation.
- **Mental Health and Self-Worth Issues:** Exploration of challenges related to low self-esteem, self-worth, and the internalized pain from unresolved familial conflicts.
- **Abandonment and Emotional Unavailability:** Discussions surrounding absent or emotionally unavailable family members and the resulting effects on relationships and mental well-being.

Please take care of your mental health while reading. If at any point you feel overwhelmed, remember that it's okay to pause and return to the material later. Seeking support from trusted individuals, mental health professionals, or support groups is encouraged if you find yourself affected by these topics.

Your well-being is important.

CONTENTS

-

INTRODUCTION

Writing this book began with confronting a difficult truth in my life: my battle with addiction and it's undeniable connection to the relationship I have with my father. For years, I struggled with my self-worth, actions of self-abuse and what felt like profound moments of lacked self-care. In my attempts to eradicate those behaviors, I began to understand they stemmed from deeper emotional wounds which were created by the fractured bond between my father and I. While not every broken father-son relationship will result in addiction or self-destruction, my journey has taught me just how profound the impact of this relationship, or its lack thereof, can be on our sense of self, our partnerships and relationships, and our overall ability to heal.

Writing this book has been one of my truest acts of self-care and a genuine process of my healing. The journey of revisiting some of the darkest moments in my childhood and adult life required me to hold up a mirror to my pain, to acknowledge the scars left behind by my emotionally distant father and to take accountable actions towards my own healing. This is not a story of blame or judgment but instead, a story of understanding the complexities of father-son relationships, the ways they can shape and mold our identities and the resilience required to break free from patterns that no longer serve us.

For years I lived in the shadow of my father's absence. I spent a significant portion of my life feeling the profound impact of him not being present; physically or emotionally. This lead to difficulty trusting or forming healthy relationships while being tied to feelings of abandonment and insecurity. Not to mention, difficulty forming a strong sense of self in adolescent years.

I often refer to the relationship with my father as the first failed relationship of my life as it created a wound that became the blueprint for every other relationship I entered. In those relationships, dishonesty, deception and infidelity weren't just patterns I encountered, they were patterns I then repeated. In my search for love, I chased the acceptance I never received while growing and perpetuating the cycle of hurt I had been born into.

In that cycle of pain, addiction became my way of numbing—numbing the rejection, the inadequacy, and the emptiness of not feeling loved or valued. But numbing doesn't heal, it only deepens the wound. It wasn't until I stopped running from the root of my pain and confronted it head-on, that I began the slow and difficult but advantageous journey toward healing.

Along this journey through therapy, self-reflection and support, I've come to understand that healing isn't about erasing the past. Alternatively, it's about learning to live with your past in a way that removes it's burden and instead, moves you towards empowerment. In applying this understanding to my own past associated with my father, I've learned that the bond between father and son is sacred but also fragile. When nurtured, it has the power to transform lives but when broken, it can leave behind a legacy of pain that ripples across generations.

This book is your invitation to heal. Is it for anyone who has felt the weight of a broken bond or the longing for connection. This book is my testament to the power of resilience and the potential for growth, no matter how far down a destructive path you may go. My goal is to offer new fathers, current fathers and sons in pain, a deeper understanding of the natural bond between father and son and the tools to repair it, if needed. This bond, though complicated and imperfect, has the potential to heal, to inspire and to create a brighter future.

To those reading this, your pain is not the end of your story—it is the beginning of your strength. You are not defined by the love you lacked or the mistakes you've made but instead, by the courage it takes to choose the often difficult path of healing. This journey is for you, for the legacy you will create and the lives you will touch. Whether through rebuilding a relationship, finding peace within yourself or inspiring change in others, there is always room for growth and hope for a brighter and more compassionate path forward. Healing is a choice and your next step begins here.

1

THE FOUNDATION OF

FATHERHOOD

The father-son relationship is one of the deepest bonds a person can experience. It's the foundation from which sons build their knowledge and understanding of masculinity, trust, and emotional stability. Fathers who are actively involved and present in their sons' lives, providing a safe space for discovery and growth, enable their sons to develop confidence and a sense of self-worth. This connection is not just a biological one; it is a dynamic relationship that shapes how sons view themselves and their place in the world. By cultivating this relationship, fathers become important agents in their sons' emotional and psychological lives that shape their later relationships and interactions.

This understanding of the father-son bond has not always come easily to me. In fact, my own relationship with my father was, and is, fractured and filled with painful lessons. Addressing those very lessons and experiences are what allowed me the ability to write this book. It's not the easiest story, but its relevance has helped me learn the importance of father-son relationships, how to heal from its loss, evolve from its disappointment, and eventually, understand the truest nature of its significance.

For the vast majority of my childhood, my father was absent. And when he was around, he wasn't the man I needed him to be. He wasn't a consistent role model or a source of comfort. To be frank, when he was present, he was volatile and often verbally and physically abusive. The relationship between he and my mother was a prime example of that. Their relationship was the first relationship I ever witnessed and it was one of violence and confusion. I saw my father hurt my mother in every way imaginable—verbally, physically, mentally and even sexually. As a child, I didn't fully understand it, and although I instinctively knew it was wrong, I also saw my mother stay which caused me to believe, that relationships like that, were normal. The mixed signals I perceived were confusing and at times, overwhelming—sometimes it seemed he loved my mother, but then he'd be cruel and mean to her. That very dynamic also extended to me as his son. When he "loved" me, he'd show pride, but when he didn't, he was harsh and abusive.

This perception skewed my understanding of love and relationships from an early age. I grew up believing that love was an unpredictable mix of tenderness and cruelty, that it was normal for love to hurt. This belief manifested in my adult life in tremendous ways, especially in romantic relationships.

I found myself staying in toxic relationships filled with deception and infidelity because, deep down, that's what I understood love to be—chaotic and painful. In therapy, I learned to unpack these experiences and understand how my childhood shaped my perception of relationships in ways that weren't healthy.

My father was no simpler in his conception of masculinity. Having come from a long line of "macho" men, my father viewed anything less as weak or "feminine". As a child, I loved to sing, dance, and perform, which didn't align with his view of what a "man" should be. I remember a specific incident quite vividly—a moment that encapsulates the perplexing and confusing relationship I had with my father. While on the subway in New York City, my father paraded me in front of his mistress because she adored the fact that I was a handsome little performer. During that moment of performance, for the first time, I felt like my father was proud of me.

For that brief moment in time, he seemed to love what I loved. It was there that I felt safe, seen, loved and accepted..

But that joy was short-lived. On another occasion, wanting to recreate that proud look on my fathers face during that subway ride, I began performing for him at home, away from the approval of others. His reaction, however, was very different. Time time around, as no one was there to impress with my performance, his true feelings showed and he wasn't happy. He despised what he perceived as the "feminine" nature of my singing and dancing and in that moment, in our cramped One bedroom apartment in New York City, he punched me in the face, knocking me unconscious — I was five years old. I woke up bewildered but with a strange clarity. Moments before the punch, I had been wholeheartedly myself—singing, dancing, smiling. In that instant, I learned that being myself was not safe. From that moment, for many years to follow, I built an armor around myself, subconsciously believing that if I showed too much of who I really was, I'd be hurt.

This memory, and others like it, shaped my view and understanding of masculinity. My father's disapproval of me, his violent reactions to vulnerability, and his inability to embrace emotional openness created a belief in me that to be man, I had to suppress my true self. That belief followed me into adulthood and took years of therapy to unlearn — a belief I still continue to unlearn.

This further plays into understanding how the relationship between fathers and sons is a pivotal role in shaping both of their futures. The earliest male role model is the father and he influences how his sons perceive masculinity, emotional expression, and relationships. By actively guiding and supporting their sons, fathers play a crucial role in shaping their values, which can lead to the development of resilience, confidence, and a strong sense of purpose in their lives. This guidance can ultimately aid in preparing sons to face life's challenges with a positive mindset and a belief in their own abilities.

But what happens when that guidance is absent? As I write throughout this book, my father's physical and emotional absence, created a void that I spent many years, unsuccessfully, trying to fill. I write, not from a place of having overcome the damage caused by our fractured relationship but instead, from a place of understanding it's deep impact. Not just on myself but on every father-son relationship.

The foundation of fatherhood isn't built overnight, and it isn't perfect. It is a journey filled with mistakes, missteps, and, hopefully, growth. The relationship I experienced with my father has, in many ways, shaped who I am today. Even though I am still actively working through the scars left by that relationship, I am grateful for the lessons it has taught me—both about myself and about the kind of father I aspire to be. It has immensely highlighted the importance of the bond shared between father and son while also teaching me what kind of father I don't want to be.

The father-son bond also extends far beyond simply the individual relationship between the two. Meaning, as fathers embrace their role in shaping their sons' futures, they contribute to a generation equipped with the emotional tools necessary for healthy relationships which also contributing to their own their generation by setting a example. Viewing positive father-son relationships encourage other fathers to actively engage in childcare and nurturing behaviors, potentially leading to a broader shift in societal expectations regarding father involvement.

I've seen this firsthand in some my close friendships. Watching men I love as brothers become fathers has been a life-changing experience. There's a unique energy when a man holds his son for the first time. It's a light that radiates—filled with pride and love. Recently, one of my closest friends became a father and the transformation in him was incredible to see. He'd always been a loving and caring man but fatherhood increased his emotional state tenfold. Spending time with he and his family recently while on holiday, I saw as he held his son with such immense joy. I also had an opportunity to be around for a beautiful and somewhat challenging moment of putting his little boy to sleep for the night. As he cradled his crying 11-month old to sleep, he exhibited great love, dedication and patience. In that moment, I saw clips of their future relationship—baseball games, arguments, laughter, and love. It was a powerful reminder of the beauty of fatherhood, and it further inspired me to reflect on my own experiences.

Ultimately, the foundation of fatherhood is about creating a safe space for sons to grow into themselves while allowing them to express who they truly are, without fear of rejection or harm. While my own experiences with my father have been difficult, they've taught me the value of healing and the importance of striving for a better version of fatherhood for the next generation.

2

THE SCIENCE OF CONNECTION

Psychological theories explain the profound depth of father-son relationships, offering insights into how early bonds influence a son's emotional and psychological development. For instance, attachment theory explains that an individual that developed a secure attachment are generally more confident in their actions, resilient and have deeper relational skills. It also explains that individuals that develop an insecure attachments may have challenges with intimacy, trust and self-worth. According to attachment theory, fathers can use their early interactions with their sons to actively build a secure attachment by being responsive to their needs with warmth, affection and care, consistently providing a safe and supportive environment and engaging in playful interactions, as the foundation for a strong bond and secure attachment is laid down in early childhood. Having an understanding of this theory can help fathers comprehend the importance of engaging meaningfully with their sons, laying a foundation of love and security that endures.

Social learning theory highlights the influence of modeled behavior. Fathers serve as primary guides, demonstrating how to manage emotions, navigate relationships and build self-perception. Sons internalize observed behaviors—whether positive or negative—and carry these lessons into adulthood. For instance, a father who demonstrates empathy and respect teaches his son to value these traits in himself and others. Conversely, a father who suppresses vulnerability may inadvertently model emotional suppression as a norm. Conscious choices allow fathers to instill enduring values like kindness and integrity, equipping their sons to thrive in an often-complex world.

These theories resonate deeply with my personal experiences. My father's version of masculinity prioritized strength over sensitivity, with rare glimpses of warmth amidst frequent withdrawal. This inconsistency created a fragile foundation of self-worth. Moments of connection offered hope, but they were overshadowed by a persistent sense of instability. My journey to untangle these early impressions has been one of understanding, healing, and redefining what it means to "be enough."

Generational trauma adds another layer of complexity and potential complications in father-son relationships. Fathers often carry unresolved struggles or emotional wounds from their own upbringing. These wounds can surface in their parenting, perpetuating cycles of abandonment, inadequacy or emotional unavailability. Recognizing this dynamic can empower fathers to seek healing—not just for themselves but for their children. By addressing their own pain, fathers have the opportunity to break these cycles, deepening their connection with their sons and fostering mutual growth.

For me, the transmission of generational trauma was evident in how my father responded to vulnerability. His actions were shaped by his own insecurities, which he unknowingly projected onto me. This dynamic was especially evident in his criticism of my sexual orientation—a deeply damaging experience that left me questioning my worth for years. His attempts to "test" my masculinity by testing my sexuality, not only instilled shame but also created a foundation of self-doubt that complicated my journey toward self-acceptance and authentic connection. These patterns, once ingrained, can take a lifetime to unlearn but they are not insurmountable.

Attachment theory suggests that early experiences with love and security—or the lack thereof—shape our approach to relationships. My parents' relationship was turbulent at best. Most days were filled with tense arguments or heavy silence, creating an environment where peace felt like an illusion. Yet one memory stands out, bright and rare against the backdrop of chaos. It occurred during a brief period of reconciliation in the cramped one-bedroom apartments we briefly lived in above a bodega in Brooklyn. The space was cluttered with hand-me-down furniture and stacks of unpacked clutter. Amid this disarray, I witnessed my father holding my mother in an unfamiliar yet genuine way, his arm wrapped around her as if he had momentarily let his guard down. The air felt thick with warmth and possibility—a rare pause in the constant storm. For just a moment, it seemed as though love could be real between them.

That fleeting moment of connection filled me with a fragile hope that things could change. Yet, like so many others, it was quickly overshadowed by the return of conflict and instability. Mixed signals like these, psychologists note, can leave lasting imprints, fostering a fear of love's impermanence. For years, I carried that fear, wondering if love, like my father's presence, could simply vanish.

Trauma isn't defined solely by harmful actions but also by the absence of critical emotional needs like security, empathy, or validation. As a child, I often wandered the streets of Brooklyn searching for something stable to hold onto. One day stands out—a moment that profoundly shaped my perception of trust and safety. Taking my normal route home, I was led astray by a stranger offering a shortcut, in an experience that shattered my innocence. Having the impressionable mind of a young child with a gained sense of independence due to absent parents, I followed the stranger pretty easily.

Within a few short blocks, I was deviated off the path home where this fully grown adult man had now exposed his genitals to me and insisted I touch him. The moment was quick and broken due to a loud noise in the street. As the stranger turned his head, I ran away as quickly as I could. Desperate for comfort, I rushed home only to find an empty apartment. My father's absence in that moment—when I needed someone to reassure me, to protect me—engrained a belief that vulnerability would inevitably lead to disappointment. This painful memory became a cornerstone of my understanding of relationships, making trust and comfort elusive concepts for much of my life.

Despite the scars left by these early experiences, healing is possible. Fathers who recognize their influence and prioritize intentional efforts—such as affirming words, and consistent presence—can profoundly reshape their sons' lives. Even in the absence of such efforts, sons can find healing through self-reflection and personal growth. In my journey, therapy has been a lifeline. Revisiting painful memories but now armed with tools to grow through them, has allowed me to confront the shame and fear that use to hold me captive. In working through the experiences, I've learned that my past doesn't have to define me. Instead, it can serve as a space for growth and transformation. In redefining my past experiences and gaining new perspective, I now see vulnerability not as a weakness but as a doorway to deeper connection and understanding.

Healthy father-son bonds can also provide an opportunity to redefine what it means to be strong. Traditional models of masculinity often emphasize physical dominance and emotional stoicism but these limiting stereotypes can be dismantled through intentional guidance. Fathers who encourage emotional intelligence and authenticity, empower their sons to embrace vulnerability as a strength, not as a weakness. With this framework in mind, continued open discussions about emotions, challenges, and insecurities will also pave the way for healthier relationships and a fuller sense of self. True masculinity lies in empathy, respect and the courage to be fully present.

Fathers and sons have the power to co-create a legacy of love through patience, empathy and intentionality. When fathers validate their sons' emotions and model the importance of open communication, they lay a foundation for emotional health that spans generations. Sons, in turn, can redefine their value independently of their fathers' actions, choosing to foster relationships grounded in respect and compassion. For those who carry the weight of absent or fractured relationships, healing may seem daunting. Yet the process of acknowledging and addressing emotional wounds can open pathways to peace.

The science of connection reminds us that relationships are not fixed; they are dynamic and ever-changing. By understanding the psychological underpinnings of attachment and social learning, we can begin to rewrite the narratives that previously defined us. For me, this meant no longer seeing my past as a barrier but instead as a bridge to a better understanding; of myself and others.

In sharing this part of my story and the lessons, I hope this message inspires others to confront their own past and unhealed wounds. As a collective, we can continue to break cycles of pain and redefine what it means to be strong while building connections that honor the humanity in us all. Through patience, reflection, and love, fathers and sons can pave a path toward a future rooted in understanding, resilience and hope.

3

NAVIGATING COMMUNICATION BARRIERS

Communication is an essential foundational building block of any relationship. In the relationship between father and son, it is crucial to building trust, love, and connection. When the foundation of communication is absent, strained, or shallow, the impact can be large and long-lasting. As my relationship with my father was marred by silence, distance, and a profound lack of emotional connection—this is a reality that shaped not just my childhood but the course of my entire life.

For my mother, breaking free from the cycle of pain took immense courage. When she finally chose to leave my father, it wasn't just a step toward her own healing but a profound shift in our family's life. She became a single mother to three children, shouldering the full weight of responsibility with unwavering resilience. My father, like many absent fathers, found a way to manipulate the judicial system, paying a mere $11 a month per child in child support—a total of just $33 for the three of us. My mother, pregnant at 16 and with no formal education, did all she could as we relied on government assistance. We grew up as "welfare kids," and that reality shaped us in ways we're still unpacking as adults.

Yet while we struggled, my father lived comfortably, caring for his new family. The stark disparity between our lives was never addressed. My father wasn't one to reach out to understand what we were going through nor did he seem to care about the emotional or physical toll his absence took on us. His silence wasn't just in a lack of words, it created a void where responsibility and compassion should have been.

As a child, although I didn't fully grasp the complexities of my parents' failing relationship, I was acutely aware of how the emotional distance between them spilled over into my personal relationship with my father. Because of their separation, he was only around a few hours a week but even those brief visits felt obligatory and devoid of genuine connection. He never asked about my dreams or fears. There were no heart-to-heart conversations, no attempts to truly know me. Those visits became my template for relationships—brief, surface-level exchanges with little substance or depth.

This lack of communication shaped how I approached relationships throughout my life. I came to expect that others would give only the bare minimum, mirroring what I experienced with my father. I believed that if I revealed too much of myself, people would lose interest—just as he had. This communication barrier became a blueprint for my relationships. Vulnerability became a risk I couldn't afford to take, and silence became my shield.

The absence of communication wasn't just about the words unsaid; it was the absence of care, concern, and understanding. My father's silence taught me that I was unworthy of meaningful relationships. This belief carried over into my adult life, where I tolerated harmful dynamics because they felt familiar. Much like the dynamic I had witnessed between my parents, love felt present but was overshadowed by pain. I came to believe that love, by its nature, was conditional and fraught with difficulty.

One pivotal memory from my childhood reinforced this belief. My father took me along to visit one of his mistresses, where he encouraged me to perform for her. In that moment, I felt something rare—I felt like my father was proud of me. But the pride I saw was conditional, tied to my performance, not my true self. Later, when I performed for him in private, the response was vastly different. Without the audience to validate my performance, he reacted with violence. The message was clear: who I truly was—singing, dancing, smiling—was unacceptable.

These experiences planted the belief that to be loved or valued, I had to hide my true self and perform a role that others found acceptable. This belief stayed with me for years, shaping how I communicated in relationships. I withheld my feelings, avoided vulnerability, and performed for approval, all the while carrying the weight of my father's silence.

Breaking these barriers required confronting the past. Therapy became a space where I could examine how my father's inability to communicate had shaped my life. I learned to challenge the narrative that vulnerability equals weakness. Slowly, I began to understand that open, honest and vulnerable communication, is not only a solid tool for connection but also a pathway to healing.

Fathers who encourage open communication with their sons, provide them with one of the greatest gifts they have to offer. It's not just about speaking but about listening—truly listening without judgment. Simple acts, like asking questions or acknowledging feelings, create a space where sons feel seen and valued. This kind of communication lays the foundation for trust and understanding, helping sons navigate their emotions and relationships with confidence.

It's important to understand that healing from a relationship built on foundations of poor communication, will take time and isn't something that will happen overnight. It is a process of healing that generally requires a lot of patience, self-awareness and a genuine commitment to change. For sons, it starts with recognizing that the silence they experienced wasn't their fault and doesn't define their worth. For fathers, it means stepping into discomfort to build the connections their sons need.

Throughout my own healing process, I've come to understand that the type of communication necessary for healing, is about being present and engaged. While these aren't qualities I learned or experienced from my father, they are qualities I've become determined to cultivate in my own relationships, both currently and in the future. In healing past my roots of non-communicative relationships, I've learned that having the courage to speak and the willingness to listen, can transform even the most fractured relationships.

In the end, communication turns silence into understanding and pain into love. For both fathers and sons alike, tough conversations may not come easily but will always be worth having. It is never too late to rewrite the narrative and create relationships built on honesty, trust, and connection.

4

THE IMPACT OF ABSENCE

The emotional and psychological development of sons can be profoundly influenced by the absence of a father figure. As sons will often turn to their fathers for guidance, support and a sense of identity, when their father is absent, whether physically or emotionally, a void is then created that can shape a son's sense of self and his relationships with others. This void often manifests as feelings of abandonment, confusion and inadequacy with effects that can extend well into adulthood.

Studies actually show that boys who grow up without an involved father figure, often face challenges in regulating their emotions, expressing vulnerability and forming secure relationships. The absence of a father figure can also distort a son's understanding of masculinity, leaving him to grapple with societal expectations without a clear model for healthy emotional expression. These sons may learn to internalize frustration and resentment, particularly if they feel abandoned or betrayed, which can complicate their ability to trust and form meaningful connections later in life.

This was the case with my own upbringing. Fore me, the absence of a consistent and nurturing presence of a father figure, left me struggling to understand what relationships were supposed to look like. I grew up believing that love was conditional— something to be earned through effort or sacrifice. This belief followed me into adulthood, where it shaped a recurring pattern of seeking validation in my relationships. I often found myself caught in cycles of connection and disconnection, mirroring the instability I experienced with my father.

One of the most prevalent patterns that emerged from my father's absence was my need for validation. Growing up, approval from my father felt shifty and reserved only for moments when I conformed to his expectations or performed in ways that benefited him. This taught me to shape myself to fit the desire of others—even if at the cost of my own authenticity. In my romantic relationships, I became highly focused on their needs, often bending over backwards to accommodate their desires while neglecting what I needed. I was convinced that if I could just be "enough," I could create the stable, unconditional love I craved but had never experienced. But no matter how much I gave, I always felt inadequate, and the relationships would inevitably unravel, leaving me with a reinforced fear of abandonment.

In friendships, this need for approval took a different form. I became a people-pleaser, always seeking to avoid conflict and putting others' needs ahead of my own. I was desperate to be liked, to feel valued, even if it meant suppressing my boundaries and desires. This behavior stemmed from my father's inconsistent love, which taught me that affection had to be earned—a lesson I carried into all my interactions.

Another deeply ingrained pattern was my fear of vulnerability. With my father, any moment of openness or authenticity was met with rejection, dismissal, or punishment. I learned early on that exposing my true self—whether through joy, pain, or creativity—was dangerous. This belief kept me guarded for years, preventing me from forming genuine connections. In romantic relationships, I hid parts of myself, afraid that revealing too much would lead to rejection. In friendships, I kept conversations light, never allowing people to see the depth of my scars. While I longed for closeness, my fears created walls that kept others at a distance.

The most painful realization, however, was how I unconsciously replicated my father's absence in my own behavior. I would withdraw emotionally, even in moments when I deeply wanted connection. In romantic relationships, I would pull away when things became too intense, creating distance as a form of self-protection. In friendships, I struggled to maintain consistency, retreating whenever I felt overwhelmed or exposed. These patterns mirrored my father's own tendency to disappear, reinforcing the cycle of absence that I had vowed to escape.

Recognizing these patterns was the first step toward breaking them. Therapy became a vital tool in helping me understand how my father's absence shaped my beliefs and behaviors. I learned to connect the dots between his choices and my own, recognizing that these behaviors were not intrinsic to who I was but were learned responses to pain and rejection. This understanding was empowering—it gave me the clarity to see that I wasn't doomed to repeat the cycle.

One of the most transformative realizations was that vulnerability, while frightening, held the key to genuine connection. I began to practice sharing my thoughts and emotions, first in safe spaces like therapy and trusted friendships and then eventually, in all areas of my life. These small acts of openness helped me rebuild my confidence and taught me that being authentic didn't have to lead to rejection. Becoming more open lead to deeper and more fulfilling relationships in my life.

Another breakthrough came from observing healthy father-son dynamics in other relationships. I saw how fathers who showed up consistently—physically and emotionally—created environments where their sons felt secure and valued. These observations gave me a new perspective on what was possible and inspired me to approach my own relationships differently. Rather than dwelling solely on what I lacked, I began to focus on cultivating presence, honesty and care in my connections.

For fathers, know that it's never too to address the impact of your absence. Acknowledging the pain caused by distance or silence is the first step toward rebuilding trust and repairing a fractured bond, however, open and honest communication is crucial. Start by creating a space where sons feel safe to express their feelings without fear of judgment or dismissal. Fathers, begin with small gestures like asking meaningful questions, sharing your own vulnerabilities and showing up consistently. These acts, though simple, can lay the groundwork for healing and connection.

For sons, it's important to recognize that your father's absence does not dictate who are are or your value to the world. Healing from the wounds of an absent father is a personal journey but it is one

39

that can lead to deep rooted growth. Committing to therapy, joining supportive communities and building trusting relationships, can provide the tools needed to confront and overcome these challenges. Creative outlets, mindfulness practices, and acts of self-compassion can also be powerful avenues for healing.

Breaking the cycle of absence requires conscious effort. It means choosing to show up—not just for others but for yourself. It means embracing vulnerability, even when it feels risky, and seeking relationships that honor your authenticity. The journey will be difficult but it will also be transformative. By addressing the impact of absence, both fathers and sons have the opportunity to rewrite their own narratives and create a bonds built on understanding, mutual respect and love.

Although the absence of a father can create wounds that echo throughout a son's life, those wounds do not have to define the future. By acknowledging the pain and consistently committing to the work necessary to heal, fathers and sons alike, can break the cycle; transforming absence into presence, disconnection into understanding and past pain into current and future love. Through this process, they have the power to co-create a brighter and more compassionate future.

5

HEALING EMOTIONAL WOUNDS

Healing emotional wounds is a deeply personal journey that is often, quite unpredictable. For sons who carry the weight of unresolved pain from their fathers, this process requires introspection and an unflinching willingness to confront painful truths. In the context of father-son relationships, these wounds run deep, generally playing a large influence in how sons view themselves while relating to the world. Healing doesn't always lead to full reconciliation or closure but it does create space for growth, self-acceptance and a future unbound by the past.

For years, I carried emotional scars left by my father's absence and rejection. In therapy, as I began to unravel the significance of the trauma experienced with my father, I began to understand the relationship with him as being my first failed relationship. Meaning, my first experience in viewing someone as untrustworthy, likely to lie or take advantage, to cause humiliation, to manipulate or potentially cause harm. From those early childhood experiences, I unknowingly constructed a pattern of mistrust. That pattern, alongside the lack of communication, accountability and emotional connection in our relationship, became the blueprint for how I approached all others. I assumed every connection would follow the same path—distance, disconnection, and eventual failure.

But healing begins with awareness. It wasn't until I began revisiting these early experiences that I saw the roots of my struggles. My father's rejection planted seeds of self-doubt that grew into behaviors and beliefs I hadn't consciously recognized. I learned to numb my pain with substances, thinking I could escape the feelings of inadequacy and shame that his absence left behind. It took confronting these behaviors to understand that they were symptoms, not solutions. My healing journey began when I stopped trying to numb my pain and started trying to understand it.

One of the most challenging yet transformative steps was revisiting the past—not to dwell on it but to uncover its impact on my present life. I had to face the memories of my father's absence and the emotional hollowness it left behind. These steps weren't about placing blame—they were about gaining clarity, and with time, I realized my father's rejection was more about his own struggles than a reflection of my worth. Understanding this allowed me to begin the process of letting go.

During those steps, I also uncovered the ways I had internalized my father's actions. I saw how his rejection influenced my fear of vulnerability, my constant need for validation and my tendency to sabotage relationships. These patterns were painful to acknowledge but they were also the key to breaking free. By naming them, I could begin to change them.

The process of healing wounds also became possible through forgiveness, which would later became a foundation of my healing journey. At first, the idea of forgiving my father was not a topic of discussion. Back then, forgiveness felt like I was excusing his actions or absolving him of accountability but eventually I grew to see forgiveness differently. I recognized that it was less about him and more about what I needed to grow and move forward. Over time, forgiving my father allowed me to release the anger and resentment I had carried for far too long. With that weight lifted, I reclaimed my power, refusing to let his absence define my life any longer.

Forgiveness wasn't limited to my father. I also had to forgive myself. For years, I blamed myself, not only for how I had internalized his rejection but also for the relationships I had knowingly and unknowingly sabotaged in that pain. My past actions weighed heavily on me and had become a constant burden that I no longer needed to carry. Releasing this self-blame was equally as liberating, if not more so, than letting go of my anger toward my father. This release allowed me to show compassion towards myself while acknowledging I was doing the best I could, with the tools I had at the time.

It's crucial to highlight, the process of healing emotional wounds doesn't always mean reconciliation, and that's okay. Although my father and I both made attempts to rebuild our relationship, I believe we each had our own limitations. While we made some progress, the deeper wounds stayed and I had to come to terms with the reality that our relationship might never be what I had hoped for.

Accepting this potential truth was painful but it also brought me a sense of freedom. I realized that healing isn't about fixing what's broken between two people; it's about finding peace within yourself, no matter the outcome.

Through this process, I began to redefine validation and self-worth. I realized I no longer needed approval from others to feel complete. I stopped performing for love and started embracing my authenticity. Vulnerability, once a source of fear, became a source of strength. By allowing myself to be seen—flaws and all—I found deeper connections than I had ever thought possible.

For fathers, the opportunity to help heal these wounds begins with presence and accountability. Showing up consistently, listening without judgment and creating a space for open dialogue can have a profound impact. Healing doesn't require perfection but it does require effort. By demonstrating vulnerability and a willingness to engage, you can help your sons to feel valued and understood.

For sons, healing is about reclaiming your narrative. Your father's actions—or inactions—do not define your worth. Healing requires patience and courage and it is possible even without reconciliation. Forgiveness—whether of your father, yourself, or both—can be a pivotal step, not because it erases the pain but because it frees you from its grip.

Healing is an ongoing journey of self-discovery alongside a process of moving forward with compassion for both yourself and others. It's about turning pain into resilience and finding deeper understanding within yourself. Whether or not your relationship with your father is ever fully mended, the true goal is to build a life where love, trust and emotional connection can grow and thrive.

A MESSAGE TO FATHERS AND SONS

To fathers: Your actions carry immense weight in your son's life. Be present, be accountable, and show your son that he is worthy of love and respect. Even small gestures of care and understanding can make a profound difference.

To sons: Your journey of healing is your own. Whether or not your father is part of that process, you have the power to break the cycle of pain. Seek support, embrace vulnerability and trust that you are worthy of love and connection.

Healing will take time, effort, dedication and courage. It's a journey worth taking that's less about erasing your past and more about finding the strength in your story. It's a journey that can lead to a life filled with understanding, compassion and the kind of love that begins from within.

6

REBUILDING TRUST AFTER

BETRAYAL

Trust is an essential part of any meaningful relationship, especially between fathers and sons. When that trust is broken—through absence, neglect or unmet needs—the effects can be felt throughout a son's life. They will be a factor in shaping his self-esteem, his relationships and his sense of stability. Rebuilding trust after such breaches is not easy, but it is possible. It requires commitment, accountability, and collaboration from both fathers and sons. By addressing the pain of the past and committing to actionable steps for change, trust can be restored, paving the way for a deeper, more resilient bond.

Rebuilding trust begins with acknowledgment. Fathers must take responsibility for the ways they have fallen short, whether through broken promises, emotional distance, or neglect. This acknowledgment must be genuine, accompanied by an openness to hear their son's perspective without defensiveness or excuses. For sons, this can be an opportunity to articulate their feelings and share how their father's actions impacted them. This process is not about assigning blame but about creating a space where both parties feel seen and understood. Honest acknowledgment lays the foundation for the trust-building process, signaling a willingness to grow and change.

Accountability is the next critical step. Trust cannot be rebuilt on words alone; it requires consistent actions that demonstrate reliability and care. Fathers can begin by following through on even the smallest commitments, such as attending events, keeping promises, or simply being present when they say they will be. These seemingly small gestures send a powerful message: "You can count on me." For sons, accountability may mean expressing their needs and boundaries clearly, creating a mutual understanding that allows the relationship to evolve with respect and openness.

Consistency is key in this process. Rebuilding trust will require dedicated time and a sustained effort. It's not about grand gestures but about showing up consistently, day after day. Fathers who demonstrate dependability reinforce the idea that they are invested in the relationship, creating a stable foundation for healing. Sons, in turn, can learn to trust their father's actions over time, allowing space for the bond to strengthen.

Shared activities provide another avenue for rebuilding trust. Whether through hobbies, projects, or simple quality time—creates opportunities for connection and shared joy. For example, a father and son might take up a new hobby together, such as hiking, sports, games, woodworking, or cooking, fostering camaraderie and creating new memories that overshadow past grievances.

Open communication remains a fundament of trust-building. Fathers and sons must prioritize honest dialogue, even when the conversations are difficult. This means creating a safe space where vulnerability is encouraged and judgment is set aside. Fathers can model this openness by sharing their own struggles, regrets, and hopes, showing their sons that they are willing to engage authentically. Sons, in turn, can use this space to express their emotions and needs, helping to dismantle barriers of misunderstanding.

Cultural and societal influences also play a role in shaping father-son dynamics. Fathers may face generational expectations or societal pressures that impact their understanding of how they engage with their sons. By reflecting on these influences, both fathers and sons can gain a deeper understanding of their relationship and approach trust-building with greater compassion. For example, a father raised with the belief that emotions should be suppressed might struggle to show vulnerability. Recognizing this cultural context can help both parties approach the relationship with empathy and patience.

Seeking external support is another tool and can be invaluable in the trust-building process. Therapy or counseling provides a neutral space where fathers and sons can work through their issues with professional guidance. These sessions can help clarify communication, address unresolved pain and establish actionable goals for rebuilding trust. Spiritual advisors, mentors, or support groups can also offer perspectives and strategies tailored to their unique circumstances.

Forgiveness will also be an essential part of rebuilding trust. For fathers, a good place to start would be forgiving yourself for past mistakes. Then allowing that forgiveness to inspire meaningful and continual change. For sons, it could mean releasing the resentment and anger that may have built up over years of hurt and disappointment. It also means forgiving yourself. Forgiveness is a powerful tool that lifts the burden of unresolved pain, allowing both to move forward with refreshed autonomy. Be patient as the it's a process that takes time but it's a powerful step toward healing and reconciliation.

Rebuilding trust is a process that will require both parties. It is a collaborative journey that requires vulnerability, effort and commitment from both fathers and sons. By working together, they can transform the relationship into one built on reciprocal respect and understanding. This process is not about perfection—it is about progress. Each step, no matter how small, brings them closer to a stronger and more meaningful connection.

Trust is the bridge that connects relationships, and restoring it takes time, dedication, and perseverance. Fathers and sons who are willing to engage in this process demonstrate a commitment to growth and connection that transcends past mistakes. Each step forward reinforces the foundation of trust and creates space for healing.

Rebuilding trust is about choosing to move forward with understanding and compassion. It is an ongoing process that demands vulnerability, consistency and collaboration. For fathers, showing up and being present sends a powerful message of love and reliability. For sons, expressing needs and working through emotions allows space for connection to flourish.

While the journey may be challenging, it does offer the opportunity to transform pain into strength and separation into closeness. By embracing this process, fathers and sons can create a relationship rooted in respect, empathy and unwavering trust—a bond that not only heals the past but will also enrich the future.

7

BEING A GREAT DAD

Being a great dad is about more than providing materially—it's about showing up consistently, emotionally and physically, and creating an environment where your son feels seen, heard, and valued. A great father nurtures emotional security and models behaviors that shape his son's present and future relationships. Reflecting on the lessons I've learned—from my father's absence to witnessing close friends step into fatherhood—has shaped my vision of what it means to be the kind of father I aspire to be.

A foundation of fatherhood is being emotionally present. A father who is emotionally available creates a safe space where his son can express himself openly without fear of judgment. Connections like this further builds trust and fosters open communication, which allow sons to share their thoughts, feelings and fears. Communicating and being emotionally available isn't about having all the answers—it's about being there to listen, to sit with discomfort if it arises and to show that you care. Fathers who model emotional resilience and vulnerability teach their sons that it's okay to feel deeply as emotions are a source of strength, not weakness.

Consistency is also part of great fatherhood. Sons need to know their fathers are reliable, both in moments of celebration and in times of challenge. Following through on commitments— whether it's attending a performance or game, offering advice, or simply showing up—is critical to fostering confidence and emotional security. Conversely, inconsistency can create feelings of abandonment or mistrust that leave lasting emotional scars. Fathers who consistently show up send a clear message: "I am here, and you matter to me."

Fathers also become role models for self-worth for their sons as the way a father views and treats himself has a profound impact on his son's development. As sons especially look to their fathers for cues on how to navigate the world and how to value themselves, a father prioritizing his own mental health, setting boundaries and practicing self-care, teaches his son that self-worth is not only important —it's essential. Conversely, a father struggling with his own self-esteem, may find it challenging to model confidence and resilience for his children

For years, despite outward successes, I struggled with my self-worth and believing that I was truly deserving of love and respect. In that mental space, I could not model self-care for others as I wasn't in practice myself. It wasn't until I began prioritizing personal self-care and self-reflection, that I started to build a healthier relationship with myself. This journey, though difficult, transformed how I approached all areas of my life. I became a better friend, partner, artist, and healer, which reshaped my vision of fatherhood. To be a great dad, you must first have a positive regard and appreciation for yourself. By understanding this, you model to your children that they, too, are deserving of love and respect.

Being a great dad also means celebrating your son's individuality. By encouraging him to pursue his passions, interests and dreams, you nurture in him a sense of confidence and independence. Fathers who celebrate their sons' achievements, whatever they are, big or small, actively strengthen and affirm their sense of self-worth, sense of belonging and their sense of acceptance. By taking the time to acknowledge milestones—whether it's a school project or a personal breakthrough—fathers show their sons that their efforts matter.

Growing up without that role model, greatly tied into my struggles with self-esteem throughout my adolescence and adult life. Those struggles were deeply tied to my early childhood relationships and understanding of love. When I didn't feel worthy, I sought validation in unhealthy ways—through work, romantic relationships or harmful habits. It wasn't until I began to understand my own value and treat myself with care that I could approach relationships, including the idea of fatherhood, in a healthier way. By valuing myself, I learned to show up authentically, offering my full presence to those I cared about.

This role will manifest uniquely for each father. For fathers navigating single parenthood or non-traditional roles, the path to being a great dad may look different but the principles remain the same. As its base, intentionality, presence and emotional availability can bridge gaps to create meaningful bonds. Finding creative ways to engage with your children, perhaps by creating new traditions, can transform even the most challenging circumstances into opportunities for connection.

If being a great dad is the goal, joint endeavors will always be one of the most effective ways to deepen the bond. Whether it's learning a new skill together or spending time doing something you both already enjoy, these moments will further deepen the connection. These shared moments could also be a father taking an interest in his son's hobbies —whether it's a love of theater, music, playing sports, building a project, or a new book series —taking an interest demonstrates love through action. These moments will not just strengthen the bond, they will build trust and create opportunities for growth.

Being a great dad also means cultivating an environment where vulnerability is seen as a strength —as compassion and empathy should be at the forefront of every father-son relationship. Sons who feel supported in expressing their emotions are more likely to develop emotional intelligence and resilience. Fathers who embrace their own emotions and model healthy expression teach their sons that it's okay to feel deeply and to seek connection through honesty and openness.

The journey to being a great dad is a journey that starts from within. If you are a father struggling with your own self-worth, know that seeking help—whether through therapy, self-care or personal reflection—is a sign of strength. The more you invest in understanding and valuing yourself, the more you can give to your children. Fathers who prioritize their own growth and well-being while demonstrating integrity and kindness, create an environment where they and their sons can thrive. In this space fathers will also inspire their sons to pursue their own personal development.

Remember, being a great dad isn't about being perfect. It's about showing up consistently, being willing to learn and growing alongside your son. By embodying qualities such as emotional availability, dependability and empathy, fathers can create a foundation of trust and care that shapes their son's life for years to come. In doing so, they teach their sons a powerful lesson: true strength lies in understanding and loving oneself.

8

BUILDING TRUST

Building trust between fathers and sons is a continuous journey, one that evolves over time and requires a deep commitment to presence, communication and understanding. Trust is not built through singular, grand gestures but in the quiet consistency of showing up, listening, and supporting your son's individuality. As a father, your role is not only to guide and mentor but also to recognize and celebrate your son for who he truly is, nurturing a relationship that fosters his growth and strengthens your bond.

Trust begins with presence. Being not only physically but emotionally available, will send a powerful message: "You matter." When sons feel valued and understood, they thrive. This sense of security also lays the groundwork for trust to flourish. The effort is more important than perfection. Whether it's enjoying a meal together, going on a walk or discussing a tough topic, these everyday moments weave the fabric of trust.

One of the most powerful tools for building trust is showing appreciation. When fathers express their gratitude, it creates a positive feedback loop that reinforces connection and understanding. This can be as simple as acknowledging the efforts of their sons—whether in be in academics, personal growth, creative expression or hobbies. For example, if your son finishes a school project or showcases an amazing performance, take a moment to celebrate his achievement and accomplishment. Or perhaps he shows interest in pursuing a new hobby like painting, learning an instrument or an interest in sports, recognize his dedication and offer assistance if needed. A heartfelt "I'm proud of you" or "I see how hard you're working" can notably boost your son's self-esteem and motivate him to strive for more. This will foster an environment where he feels valued not just for what he accomplishes but for the passion and effort he brings to into his pursuits.

Appreciation also helps bridge communication barriers that often exist between fathers and sons. In a busy world filled with distractions, a genuine conversation or a note of encouragement can become a cherished moment. Fathers who take the time to recognize their sons' strengths and interests demonstrate emotional intelligence and vulnerability. This practice not only strengthens trust but also creates a foundation for deeper, more meaningful interactions.

Bonding activities will always be a undoubtable tool for building connection and trust.

As traditional father-son bonding activities often focus on sports or physical challenges, it's important to note, not all fathers and sons share these interests. Recognizing and supporting your son's unique passions, takes additional efforts. Activities like attending a play, watching a musical performance or participating in an art class together, can create variety in your efforts to build on meaningful shared experiences. Similarly, discussing a book you've both read or working out together can foster connection through mutual growth and understanding. For sons who enjoy creative pursuits, fathers can show support by engaging with their artistic endeavors—whether that means painting alongside them, listening to the music they've composed, or simply taking an active interest in their projects. For those who thrive intellectually, participating in thought-provoking conversations, attending a lecture together, or even debating topics over dinner can create opportunities for bonding. The key is to honor your son's individuality and adapt your approach to his interests, demonstrating that you value him for who he is.

Vulnerability is also an essential component of building trust. Sharing your own struggles, challenges or lessons learned, shows your son that it's okay to be imperfect and human. It invites him to share his own experiences without fear of judgment. This mutual openness fosters emotional intimacy and deepens the father-son bond. At the same time, consistency reinforces this trust. Following through on commitments—no matter how small—signals reliability and care. Whether it's showing up for a school event, being present for a scheduled conversation, or showing up for scheduled activities, these acts communicate that your son can depend on you. Consistency creates stability, a foundation upon which trust can grow over time.

The trust you build with your son extends beyond your immediate relationship, influencing his interactions with others and shaping the values he carries forward. Fathers who model trustworthiness, empathy, and accountability set a precedent for how their sons approach their own relationships. By breaking cycles of emotional neglect or inconsistency, you create a legacy of connection and care that can positively impact future generations.

For fathers seeking to build trust and reconnect after a period of absence or disconnection, patience, humility, and intentional effort is required. Acknowledging past mistakes and taking responsibility is a critical first step. This means listening to your son's experiences and feelings, even when they're difficult to hear. Small, consistent gestures—like a weekly call, a thoughtful message, or attempts to spend time together—can demonstrate your commitment to mending the relationship. Rebuilding trust will take time but know that each step forward contributes to a stronger foundation. By consistently and authentically showing up, even in the face of resistance or setbacks, you communicate to your son that you value your relationship and are invested in its growth.

Ultimately, building trust is about being present, authentic and a displaying a willingness to grow together. Remember, it's not about perfection but about making the effort to show up, listen, and adapt. Trust is the bridge that carries fathers and sons through life's challenges, creating a bond that evolves and strengthens over time.

9

FATHER AS A ROLE MODEL

The bond shared between a father and son is a connection that deeply influences how a son perceives himself and the world. Fathers are more often than not, a son's first role model, setting examples through their words, actions and attitudes. Their influence extends far beyond the home, shaping how their sons navigate relationships, handle challenges and define their own values. A father's behavior teaches his son how to embody integrity, show compassion and approach life with resilience and purpose.

Trust is the foundation of being a role model. Sons look to their fathers for consistency and reliability, learning the importance of following through on promises and treating others with respect. When fathers are present, emotionally available, and accountable, they teach their sons to value authenticity and dependability in their own relationships. This foundation encourages sons to build connections rooted in trust and mutual understanding.

As I worked through painful memories and confronted my own pain, I began questioning what it meant to be a father and to be a man. I didn't want my own masculinity to mean strength without compassion or love that came with conditions. It made me reconsider the type of man I wanted to be. My father's influence taught me all the things I didn't want to become.

True masculinity, I realized, isn't about physical power or financial status. It's about emotional strength, compassion, vulnerability, and the courage to understand rather than judge. My father's failures taught me these things in a roundabout way, showing me the necessity of kindness, patience and openness in a man's life. This redefinition became clearer as I observed friends who became fathers, men who displayed love for their children that wasn't conditioned on meeting expectations. Watching them interact with their children showed me the kind of father I could be, even if I didn't have that model growing up. This understanding allowed me to redefine my sense of masculinity, to find strength not in hiding pain but in confronting it, not in imposing judgment but in offering acceptance.

Fathers who model emotional intelligence create a lasting impact on their sons' development. This begins with demonstrating vulnerability and openness. For example, sharing personal experiences —whether about overcoming failure, navigating tough decisions, or showing kindness in difficult circumstances—teaches sons that strength lies in being honest about one's feelings and actions. A father who shows his son that it's okay to feel deeply and make mistakes, offers an invaluable lesson in resilience and self-acceptance.

Fathers who continually model self-improvement, will also encourage their sons to embrace growth and adaptability. By openly pursuing their own personal development—whether through therapy, fitness, education, or mindfulness practices—fathers demonstrate that learning and evolving are lifelong endeavors. This approach helps sons understand that it's not only okay to seek help or change course but that doing so is an essential part of building a fulfilling and meaningful life.

One of the most powerful ways fathers act as role models is by embodying the values they hope to instill as their sons learn not just from what they say but from what they do. For example, a father treating others with kindness and respect demonstrates the importance of dignity in everyday interactions. Similarly, fathers who handle conflicts constructively—through listening, patience, and compromise—teach their sons the value of effective communication and empathy. Lessons are not just taught through lectures but through lived experiences, observed and absorbed by sons as they grow.

Modeling perseverance is another crucial role fathers play. Life inevitably presents challenges, and how a father approaches adversity shapes how his son perceives resilience. A father who faces obstacles with determination and problem-solving tactics, teaches his son the importance of persistence. Whether it's completing a challenging project, supporting loved ones through difficult times, or pursuing personal growth, these examples of perseverance become a blueprint for sons to follow in their own lives.

Modeling individuality and emotional support is another important factor and can be done by incorporating diverse bonding activities. Shared activities naturally strengthen the bond between father and son, but going beyond traditional pursuits allows fathers to engage in experiences that nurture creativity and encourage intellectual growth. Attending a play or performance, collaborating on an art project, or sharing thoughts on a favorite book provides moments that nurture both connection and mutual learning. These activities emphasize that bonding is not confined to physical or competitive experiences but can thrive in spaces of shared curiosity and creativity.

For instance, a father who embraces his son's love for music—by attending his recital, discussing his favorite genre, or even exploring a music class together—demonstrates the importance of valuing personal interests. Similarly, working on a shared project like building something meaningful or volunteering together fosters a sense of collaboration and responsibility. These moments create more than just positive memories; they teach lessons about mutual respect, commitment, and the pride that comes from working toward a shared goal. By adapting activities to align with their son's unique passions, fathers not only strengthen their bond but also celebrate the diversity of their relationship.

Fathers who are also aware of how to thoughtfully navigate cultural expectations, model a broader definition of masculinity. Cultural perceptions of masculinity—centered on stoicism and dominance—can generally limit emotional expression while building obstacles, making it difficult to connect. Fathers who challenge these stereotypes by embracing qualities like compassion, creativity, and emotional vulnerability, pave the way for their sons to experience a more full and authentic version of masculinity.

Fathers who redefine masculinity through compassion and openness create a model for their sons to follow. My father's actions, or lack thereof, pushed me to explore my own understanding of masculinity, leading me to conclude that true strength lies in vulnerability, in being able to show love without conditions, and in having the courage to face and express emotions. As I worked to redefine what it means to be a man and a father, I found role models in unexpected places—among friends who parented with love, and in myself as I sought to embody the values I had longed to see in my father.

The ripple effect of a father's example is profound. Sons who grow up observing integrity, kindness, and emotional intelligence in their fathers carry these values into their own relationships, shaping their interactions with partners, friends, and colleagues. The lessons imparted by a father resonate through the generations, influencing not just his son but the family and community his son builds in the future. Fathers have the unique ability to create a legacy of love and respect by embodying the principles they wish to pass on.

The lessons imparted by a father resonate through the generations, influencing not just his son but the family and community his son builds in the future, with partners, friends and colleagues. Fathers have the unique ability to create a legacy of love and respect by embodying the principles they wish to pass on.

Ultimately, being a role model as a father is about showing up, being present and demonstrating values through everyday actions. Fathers who prioritize emotional availability, honesty and growth, create an environment where their sons can thrive. By choosing to lead with kindness, courage, and empathy, they teach their sons that manhood is not about meeting societal expectations but about becoming a compassionate and authentic individual who is unafraid to face life's challenges with integrity and heart.

10

STRENGTHENING THE BOND

Strengthening the bond between a father and son requires intentionality, emotional vulnerability and experiences that cultivate trust. Creating moments that resonate, teach, and heal, while at times may sometimes be challenging, with commitment, can also be incredibly rewarding. This chapter explores how fathers and sons can deepen their relationship by addressing emotional wounds, embracing shared moments, and fostering growth through compassion and understanding.

Building a strong bond goes beyond the activities themselves; it's about the connection built in the process. Whether through quiet conversations, moments of laughter, or simply being present together, these interactions provide opportunities to better understand one another on a deeper level. Exploring a son's unique interests or passions creates space for individuality to shine, showing that a father values his son for who he truly is. It's not about the specific task at hand but the intentional effort to create a relationship rooted in care and mutual respect. These moments offer a foundation where trust can flourish, emotions can surface naturally, and the father-son relationship becomes a safe space for growth and understanding.

What makes shared experiences truly impactful is the vulnerability they invite. Engaging in activities together allows emotions to surface in a way that feels natural, not forced. For example, a father who teaches his son to cook may find that the conversation shifts from ingredients to more personal matters—like a tough day at school or a lingering fear.

The act of focusing on a task together provides a buffer, making it easier to broach sensitive topics.

During my recovery journey, I found that connection wasn't always about grand gestures. A simple conversation during a walk or a shared silence while painting could create the emotional space needed to process pain. In one group therapy session, a father and son shared how they had reconnected by restoring an old car. While fixing the engine, they also repaired their communication. What struck me most was how the son described the experience: "It wasn't about the car. It was about having my dad's attention and knowing I mattered." Fathers have a unique ability to create these moments, but it requires a willingness to be present and emotionally available. Vulnerability doesn't mean having all the answers—it means showing up, listening, and sometimes admitting you don't have all the answers. It's in these raw moments that trust is rebuilt and strengthened.

In our evolving understanding of father-son dynamics, it's essential to move beyond traditional bonding activities like sports or outdoor adventures. While these remain valuable, fathers can expand their repertoire to include creative and intellectual pursuits. Attending a play, exploring an art exhibit, or even taking a dance class together celebrates individuality and encourages self-expression.

Another transformative experiences I witnessed was a father and son participating in a pottery class. The son, a teenager, had initially been reluctant, saying it wasn't very "manly". Yet, as they worked on their creations side by side, I overheard the boy sharing stories from his day, opening up in a way that seemed very different from the impression I first got of him at the start of the class. It wasn't the clay that mattered anymore—it was the connection forged in that moment. Moments like these remind us that bonding is about shared effort and mutual interest, not conformity to societal expectations.

For fathers and sons who may feel disconnected, shared activities offer a tangible way to communicating and start the healing process. It's not about finding the perfect activity; it's about the intention behind it. In therapy one father shared how he and his adult son began reconnecting through monthly cooking nights. He shared that at first, their conversations were surface-level, but over time, they started discussing deeper topics—dreams, regrets, and even forgiveness. The act of cooking became a ritual that symbolized their effort to rebuild their relationship. Their story is a testament to the power of consistent, intentional effort in transforming a bond.

Strengthening the bond also requires acknowledging and addressing deeper emotional wounds. For many, these wounds stem from feelings of abandonment, misunderstanding and/or betrayal. Confronting these emotions head-on, rather than avoiding them, is essential for healing and growth.

For me, the absence of a nurturing father during my childhood and young adult life, left a void I unknowingly sought to fill elsewhere, often in self-destructive ways. Drug usage and eventual addiction became my way of numbing emotions I couldn't face. It wasn't about seeking thrill or escape; it was about avoiding the pain I had buried deeply. My journey to recovery began with confronting this pain, understanding its roots and from there, learning to feel again.

Confronting my pain did also take me acknowledging I hit rock bottom, which doesn't always look like what we'd expect. For me, it wasn't just losing a job or a relationship—it was feeling nothing. That numbness became my reality, cutting me off from my core values of connection and creativity. Recovery wasn't a quick fix; it was a gradual return to myself. Through therapy, support groups, and honest self-reflection, I began to rebuild my sense of worth, realizing that my value couldn't be measured by external validation but had to come from within.

During that time, I often found myself reflecting on my upbringing—not to assign blame, but to gain insight and learn how to grow beyond the experiences I was still holding onto with anger. It was during those moments that I began sifting through my memories, searching for the 'good moments' I had shared with my father. Although I lacked many shared experiences, one memory stands out: the first time he met my ex-fiancé. It was a vulnerable moment where he showed a genuine desire to connect with my partner. This interaction disempowered some of the anger and resentment I had carried regarding our relationship and his views on my orientation. While our bond remained distant, that moment revealed his potential for connection, teaching me that even brief instances of vulnerability can begin to bridge divides.

In recovery, I learned to find meaning in the connections I could build. One day, a friend invited me to volunteer at a community event, planting trees with a group of young boys. Though I was there as a mentor, I found myself learning just as much as they did. Watching them dig into the earth, asking questions about the environment, and sharing stories about their lives reminded me of the importance of being present. That day wasn't about perfection; it was about showing up and being part of something bigger than myself. It was a moment of healing—not just for them, but for me.

The father-son relationship is a journey of connection and growth, requiring effort, adaptability, and mutual understanding. Strengthening this bond means being present, fostering trust, and creating a safe space for emotions to surface naturally. For me, strengthening the bond was about learning to move past the anger. Moments like those between my father and my ex allowed me to see my father in a more human light, helping me release some of the resentment I had carried for so long. It's also about broadening your connections beyond the father-son dynamic. Building new relationships and engaging with others can offer fresh perspectives, helping to release old pain and invite new life into your journey. By embracing these opportunities, we create space for growth, healing, and deeper understanding.

As I reflect on my own journey, I see these moments as bridges—connections that span the gaps of misunderstanding, distance and pain. They are not just about what we do but about how we show up for each other. Fathers, your presence matters. Sons, your voice matters. Together, you can create a bond that not only heals but inspires. It's in these experiences that you will find the strength to navigate life's challenges and the joy of truly knowing and being known by one another.

11

CULTURAL INFLUENCES ON FATHER-SON DYNAMICS

Cultural expectations shape the dynamics of father-son relationships in profound ways, often dictating how fathers and sons perceive their roles and interact with one another. Societal norms, deeply embedded in tradition and generational beliefs, frequently influence ideas about masculinity, emotional expression, and familial responsibilities. While these norms can offer structure and identity, they may also create barriers, hindering emotional openness and authentic connections. For fathers and sons, understanding and challenging these expectations can be the key to fostering a more meaningful and resilient relationship.

In many cultures, fathers have often been seen as providers and protectors, representing strength, authority and emotional restraint. Sons, in turn, are often expected to follow suit by adopting a similar approach to manhood. While these more traditional roles may have served a purpose in the past, they can be limiting in today's world, where emotional expression and vulnerability are essential for creating and maintaining deeper connections. A father who was raised to suppress his feelings may find it difficult to create a space where his son feels safe sharing his own emotions. This gap can lead to misunderstandings, resentment, and a strain on trust within their relationship.

Fathers who challenge societal norms by embracing vulnerability and encouraging emotional dialogue model a healthier and more balanced version of masculinity. Sons who witness this openness benefit by learning that strength and sensitivity are not mutually exclusive but complementary aspects of personal growth. This 'changed mindset' begins with intentional conversations where fathers invite their sons to share their thoughts, fears and aspirations. These dialogues will not only deepen their bond but also dismantle stereotypes that have long confined men to rigid roles. Fathers who embody these qualities demonstrate that masculinity is not defined by toughness alone but by the courage to connect authentically.

Cultural influences on father-son relationships vary widely across communities and traditions. In collectivist cultures where family and community come first, fathers often focus on what's best for everyone, not just themselves. They may work hard to create a legacy or achieve goals that benefit the whole family or group, rather than pursuing personal dreams. Their role is often about providing for and protecting the family, keeping traditions alive, and ensuring the group stays strong and connected. While this can create a sense of unity, it might also mean less focus on individual emotions or personal needs, as the group's success is seen as more important. In contrast, individualist cultures focus on personal success and self-expression. People are encouraged to pursue their own goals, make their own choices and stand out as individuals, as being true to oneself are often seen as more important than following group expectations or traditions. Both frameworks offer unique challenges and opportunities for fostering connection. Fathers who navigate these cultural nuances thoughtfully can empower their sons to embrace their identities while honoring their heritage. Rituals such as celebrating holidays, passing down stories, or participating in family customs create opportunities for connection and continuity. However, as society evolves, so too must these traditions.

By embracing understanding and adaptability, fathers have a unique chance to blend cultural traditions with modern values, allowing them to honor their heritage while staying connected to today's world. For instance, a father might modernize a family tradition by incorporating his son's interests. If the family has always celebrated a specific holiday with a feast, the father could invite his son to co-create the menu, blending traditional dishes with new recipes. This collaborative effort not only honors the family's history but also allows the son to feel invested in the tradition, creating a deeper sense of connection.

While in preparation for writing this book, one father I spoke with described how he and his son reimagined a traditional rite of passage. Instead of following the rigid steps prescribed by their community, they worked together to create a ceremony that reflected their shared beliefs. This experience not only strengthened their bond but also demonstrated that cultural values can evolve to include authenticity and personal significance.

For me, growing up I often felt the tension between honoring cultural expectations and carving out my own path. While I may have admired the strength and resilience the men in my family embodied, I also longed for role models where emotional vulnerability and creativity were equally valued. This tension shaped my understanding of masculinity, teaching me that tradition and individuality don't have to be opposing forces. Instead, they can coexist, creating a richer and more nuanced relationship between fathers and sons.

I remember one family gathering, I witnessed an uncle share a deeply personal story about his struggle to balance work and family. His vulnerability, in a room where stoicism was often the norm, sparked a conversation that redefined our understanding of masculinity. This moment showed me that dismantling long-held cultural norms doesn't require dramatic actions—it begins with honesty and connection. Fathers and sons can benefit from these everyday acts of openness, where tradition meets transformation, and genuine dialogue becomes a catalyst for change.

The absence of a father figure or active engagement can also have profound cultural implications. Sons who grow up without a present or engaged father may seek guidance and validation from other sources—whether mentors, friends or community leaders. While these relationships can provide support, the absence of a father's influence often leaves a gap in how sons perceive masculinity and relationships. Fathers who seek to rebuild connections with their sons must address the cultural weight of their absence by showing empathy, consistency and a willingness to reframe the narrative. This could mean introducing traditions or rituals that weren't part of the relationship before, offering a renewed sense of identity and belonging.

Fathers who embrace emotional growth and challenge cultural norms inspire their sons to do the same. By modeling qualities like compassion, curiosity, and vulnerability, fathers redefine what it means to be a man. This transformation fosters a deeper bond between fathers and sons, creating a relationship built on mutual respect and shared growth. My journey with these cultural influences has taught me that dismantling outdated norms is a gradual but rewarding process. It requires intentionality, self-awareness, and a willingness to redefine what matters most in the father-son bond.

Ultimately, balancing tradition and individuality is not just about preserving or eliminating the past; it's about creating a future where both ideals can thrive. Fathers who adapt their roles to include emotional availability, curiosity and flexibility, pave the way for deeper connections with their sons. Sons, in turn, benefit from seeing their fathers embrace growth and vulnerability, learning that masculinity is not about conforming to a societal expectation but about living authentically. By challenging outdated norms and fostering open communication, fathers and sons not only strengthen their relationship but also contribute to a broader redefinition of masculinity and connection. This evolution is not just about breaking free from the past —it's about building a future where fathers and sons can thrive as partners, mentors and friends.

12

THE JOURNEY TO REPAIR

The journey to repair a father-son relationship is rarely linear. It requires patience, vulnerability and a willingness to confront painful truths as years of miscommunication, absence or emotional distance often leave a trail of unresolved feelings. Acknowledging the need for repair is the first step, a pivotal moment when both fathers and sons recognize that their connection—though strained— deserves an honest attempt at healing.

For many, this recognition begins with self-reflection. Fathers must evaluate their role and behaviors, asking themselves hard questions: Have they truly been present? Have they listened without judgment? Similarly, sons must confront their expectations and emotional needs. This introspection often illuminates the underlying issues shaping the relationship. By identifying these barriers, fathers and sons can articulate their desires for a more meaningful bond.

My own journey to repair my relationship with my father has been anything but straightforward. For much of my life, I believed the emotional distance and silence between us were simply a reality I had to accept. It wasn't until my struggles in adult relationships mirrored the emotional absence I experienced with my father that I realized the depth of its impact.

In my journey, therapy became a space where I unpacked the ways this relationship influenced my sense of trust, vulnerability, and emotional security. I began to see the patterns I had carried into adulthood—not just in romantic relationships, but in how I approached connections with others and with myself. While therapy helped me address these patterns, it also revealed that healing doesn't necessarily mean fixing the relationship. Sometimes, healing is about finding closure within oneself.

Fathers and sons must understand that repair is not a one-sided effort. It requires open dialogue and a shared commitment to change. Fathers should create space for their sons to express their feelings freely, validating their experiences without defensiveness. Sons, in turn, can approach these conversations with honesty, sharing their emotions without the fear of judgment. These exchanges pave the way for rebuilding trust, a cornerstone of any healthy relationship.

Rebuilding also demands accountability. Fathers may need to acknowledge moments where they fell short, offering genuine apologies that demonstrate a willingness to grow. Sons, too, must reflect on their own actions and expectations, recognizing where misunderstandings or assumptions may have contributed to the strain. This shared ownership shifts the focus from blame to collaboration, fostering a partnership rooted in mutual respect.

The Journey to repair is a journey marked by setbacks and breakthroughs. Fathers and sons must allow themselves and each other to navigate this path at their own pace. This patience will teach resilience while reinforcing the value of the relationship they are working to repair.

Through my experience with my father, I've learned that setting boundaries is essential to navigating the path toward healing. Early in my journey, I attempted weekly conversations, hoping they would lead to deeper discussions and, eventually, reconciliation. Instead, these exchanges felt surface-level and unfulfilling—a reminder that connection cannot be forced. I realized that maintaining these calls out of obligation rather than mutual desire was an emotional burden I no longer wished to carry. Choosing to step back was an act of self-preservation, a way to honor my need for authenticity.

Eventually, I released the expectation that my father and I would find resolution. That decision, although difficult, became one of my most liberating moments. This shift wasn't about giving up—it was about reclaiming my energy and redirecting it toward personal growth. For years, I carried resentment for the ways my father's absence shaped my life and forgiveness was long overdue. Letting go of that anger wasn't about excusing his actions but about releasing the hold they had on me. Forgiveness became a gift I gave myself, allowing me to move forward with clarity and peace.

It's important to acknowledge that although some fractured bonds mends, not every father-son relationship will find resolution, and that's okay. The goal is not always to mend the bond but to learn how to live and thrive despite its imperfections. Healing is about finding peace within ourselves while recognizing that we can carry the lessons of the past without being defined by them. My relationship with my father remains strained, but the work I've done to heal has shaped me into a better partner, friend, and man. I've learned the value of setting boundaries, prioritizing my mental health, and cultivating connections rooted in mutual respect.

Ultimately, the journey to repair is not just about the relationship shared between father and son —it's about the journey we take within ourselves. Whether the bond is mended or remains broken, healing will always be an act of self-love and self-discovery. Fathers and sons who take this journey together can rebuild their relationship on a foundation of understanding and mutual respect. Even if their paths eventually diverge, the lessons gained along the way leave a lasting impact.

13

THE SPIRITUAL CONNECTION

Spirituality in father-son relationships opens a pathway to deeper understanding, healing, and connection that transcends the physical and emotional realms. It invites both fathers and sons to reflect on their beliefs, values, and emotions while fostering a bond that moves beyond surface-level interactions. Through shared spiritual practices such as meditation, prayer, or time spent in nature, fathers and sons can create moments of connection. Sharing in these experiences offer opportunities to express vulnerabilities, explore aspirations and cultivate trust.

For fathers, spirituality often becomes a guiding light that helps their sons navigate life's complexities. When fathers share their spiritual practices or beliefs, they provide sons with tools to explore their own sense of purpose and identity. The process of sharing encourages open dialogue, where questions are welcomed and answers are sought together. Spirituality, offering countless benefits, also serves as a bridge between generations, creating a shared language for discussing moral dilemmas, life challenges and personal growth.

However, spirituality is not just about alignment—it is also about celebrating individuality. Fathers and sons may approach spirituality in different ways, yet still find meaningful common ground. A father who finds solace in prayer, for instance, may connect with his son by exploring mindfulness or nature-based rituals that resonate with the son's perspective. These shared practices become a space where both can honor their unique journeys while cultivating mutual respect.

My own relationship with spirituality grew as I began to understand it was a way to process the emotional void left by my father's absence. I can vividly remember one of the first times, with understanding, that I felt connected to something greater than myself. It was during a sound healing session, where the resonance of the instruments seemed to quiet the noise within me. In that moment of stillness, I realized that healing wasn't just about repairing broken relationships—it was about finding peace within. Spirituality became a way to explore my emotions without judgment, offering clarity and grounding that I had long sought.

For fathers and sons seeking reconciliation, spirituality can be a powerful tool. Reflective practices such as journaling, meditation, or guided prayer allow fathers to confront their fears, regrets, and hopes, enabling them to approach their sons with authenticity. Sons, in turn, may find that spiritual exploration helps them articulate feelings they had long buried. Together, these practices create a non-judgmental space where both can share their truths and rebuild trust. Fathers who take steps toward spiritual growth will also model resilience and accountability, inspiring their sons to embark on their own journeys of self-discovery.

Spiritual advisors can also play a transformative role in navigating father-son dynamics. Whether through counseling, mentorship, or ceremonial practices, advisors offer guidance that bridges emotional and spiritual divides. I think back to one particular spiritual retreat I was a guest at, where a father and son were also guests. This retreat included several daily activities, meditations and shared reflections. I saw over the course of three days, how the experience allowed them to communicate in ways they had never attempted before, breaking down walls of resentment and opening pathways for understanding. The son later shared that it wasn't the specific practices that mattered most, but the shared intention to heal and connect.

For sons who have experienced the absence of a father, spirituality can provide a pathway to resilience and self-acceptance. Exploring personal beliefs, connecting with mentors, or engaging in community-based spiritual practices can fill the void left by a fractured relationship. These experiences remind sons that healing and connection are possible, even when the father-son bond feels irreparable. Spirituality becomes a compass, guiding them toward relationships that nurture their growth and well-being.

Ultimately, the spiritual connection between fathers and sons is about creating a shared sense of purpose by engaging in meaningful conversations, embracing vulnerability and setting aside judgment all while honoring individual journeys. For fathers, spirituality offers a way to lead by example, showing sons that strength comes from self-awareness and a willingness to grow. For sons, it provides a space to explore their identities and values with curiosity and openness. The journey of exploring spirituality together is not just transformative—it can be a powerful tool in cultivating a bond that can withstand the test of time.

14

FUTURE PERSPECTIVES

Fatherhood is not only a responsibility but it's also an opportunity for fathers and sons to lay the foundation for future family dynamics while taking part in shaping the next generation. As I reflect on my own journey and the complicated relationship I share with my father, one truth stands out: healing starts from within. In confronting our pain and taking responsibility over our actions, we open the door to real change—both for ourselves and for the people we care about.

Throughout my adult life, I have learned to approach my parents' journey with empathy.

Becoming parents as teenagers thrust them into immense responsibility, often without the tools to navigate their own growth. Recognizing this has allowed me to release resentment for what they "did" or "didn't do." Instead, I chose to focus on the lessons their experiences have taught me, recognizing that holding onto animosity only hinders my growth. Letting go of what no longer serves us and embracing what propels us forward have become the true foundations of healing.

My upbringing and experiences has taught me that the bond between parents and their children is sacred and should be nurtured, cherished, and above all, valued. Yet, I know firsthand how easy it is to lose sight of that bond when we are caught in our own struggles. With that said, the bond particularly between fathers and sons is fragile. Left untended, it can falter under the weight of unresolved pain and missed opportunities. I've seen the damage caused by the absence of emotional support, by unresolved pain, and by the inability to communicate effectively. In my own life, I've felt where emotional distance and silence created a void that shaped my understanding of love and trust. However, I've also learned that preparing for the next generation doesn't require a perfectly healed past. It demands intentionality in how we approach the future. My own relationship with my father remains a work in progress, and as I've mentioned throughout this book, I don't write this from a place of healed perfection but rather from an ongoing journey of self-discovery and growth.

As the world evolves, so too do the dynamics of fatherhood. It's inspiring to witness individuals confront their wounds, challenge outdated norms, and intentionally choose healing. This transformation contributes to a broader societal shift, where vulnerability and emotional connection are seen as strengths rather than weaknesses. At the heart of this change are the individuals doing the inner work on themselves. Only by doing the work internally can we hope to influence others positively.

Though I am not yet a father, my life's work has taught me the value of responsibility and connection. I've learned to show up as a friend, son, brother, and partner, even when it's challenging. Through these roles, I've developed a deeper understanding of the values I want to uphold: accountability, communication, and emotional availability. These qualities are my response to the patterns I witnessed growing up—patterns of avoidance, control, and emotional distance. While I may not fully know the challenges of fatherhood, I know the importance of presence, love and support.

Whether through direct involvement or through absence, fathers shape how their sons navigate relationships, express emotions, and understand their place in the world. This truth has been a powerful mirror for me, revealing both the impact of my father's emotional distance and my own tendencies in relationships. I often reflect on the phrase "hurt people hurt people" because I have lived it and have been on both sides—someone who has been hurt and someone who has caused pain. At times, I unconsciously carried the emotional distance and avoidance I experienced with my father into my own relationships. It wasn't until I made a conscious effort to take responsibility for my actions and committed to the deeper work of healing that I began to notice a meaningful shift in how I connected with others.

Witnessing my friends becoming fathers also added a layer of awareness to my healing journey. In these friends, I see a new generation of men who are more attuned to the emotional needs of their children. One vivid memory that continues to inspire me is seeing a close friend holding his newborn son, radiating an energy so pure it was almost palpable. The pride, love, and sheer joy he exuded in that moment made me realize that fatherhood is about more than just providing—it's about showing up in ways that truly matter. This is the vision of fatherhood I aspire to, whether or not it becomes part of my legacy in a traditional sense. My healing, the work I've done, and my understanding of the bond between father and son—these are the legacies I hope to pass down.

I recognize that it takes a community to uphold these values and I am grateful for the support I have. My family, my partner, my friends, my brothers—each has played a role in keeping me aligned and encouraging me to be my best self. This support system is essential not just for me but for anyone seeking to grow and heal. Whether I'm showing up as a friend, a partner, a brother, a son, or perhaps one day as a father, I know that the people around me will continue to guide me and help me navigate the challenges and beauty of these roles.

The bond between fathers and sons extends beyond shared bloodlines—it's built on values, love, and lessons that shape us. While fathers undoubtedly influence their sons, sons also have the power to chart their own paths, choosing growth and connection over lingering resentment. Healing these bonds creates ripples of transformation, not just within families but throughout communities.

Growth is never easy but it is always a choice. For me, that choice has meant accepting that my father and I may never fully reconcile. Yet, this acceptance has fueled my journey, reminding me that healing doesn't require a perfect resolution. It's about embracing forgiveness, finding peace within, and continuing forward with hope and intention.

15

FORGIVENESS AND CLOSURE

Forgiveness is often portrayed as an act of releasing someone else from the burden of their actions but it's layers are more deeper than that. Forgiveness is about making a conscious choice, for yourself, to let go of your past pain. With its release, you are deciding that it no longer holds the power to define our present or dictate our future. For sons, it means finding the strength to forgive a father's absence, mistakes, or the pain he may have inflicted. Most importantly, it also involves the ability to forgive ourselves—for the ways we may have internalized that pain and for the negative patterns we've carried as a result.

The journey of forgiveness isn't just a single moment but a series of choices. It's a continuous process that's complex and deeply personal, requiring introspection, self-compassion, and resilience. For me, the theme of forgiveness has been central to my healing journey, shaping the way I relate to my father, to others, and most importantly, to myself. For many years, I harbored resentment toward my father. I was angry about the ways in which he was absent, emotionally unavailable, and unable to provide the kind of support I needed growing up. This anger was not just directed at him but also turned inward, manifesting as feelings of inadequacy and mistrust. It was easier to blame him than to confront the deeper truth: that I was hurt, that I felt abandoned, and that I carried those wounds into every other relationship I formed.

Forgiving my father was not an easy decision, nor was it a simple or straightforward process. I had to come to terms with the fact that he might never change, that he might never be the father I needed him to be. But holding onto that anger was like carrying a heavy weight—it was exhausting, and it kept me tethered to the past. In letting go of that burden, I was able to move forward. Forgiveness, in this sense, was a deliberate decision to release feelings of resentment and to acknowledge that he did the best he could with the tools he had, even if those tools were flawed. It was about accepting that he was a man with his own struggles, shaped by his own upbringing, and that his failures were not a reflection of my worth. This understanding allowed me to see him through a lens of empathy rather than judgment, and it gave me the space to begin healing.

While forgiving my father was a crucial step, it was only part of the journey. Perhaps the most challenging and transformative aspect of my healing process was learning to forgive myself. For so long, I had blamed myself for the ways in which our relationship had failed. Throughout my youth and young adult life, I unknowingly internalized his absence as a sign that I wasn't enough, that there was something inherently wrong with me. These feelings of inadequacy followed me into adulthood and permeated every part of my life, not limited to how I saw myself but also, how in how I allowed others to treat me.

My journey to self-forgiveness was about unlearning those negative patterns. It required me to confront the ways in which I had contributed to my own pain—by accepting relationships that were unfulfilling, by not setting boundaries and by seeking validation from others instead of from within. This was not an easy process, as it meant acknowledging my own shortcomings. However, it was also an act of self-compassion, a way of telling myself that I deserved better and that I was worthy of love and respect, even if I hadn't always believed it.

One practice that helped me sustain forgiveness was writing unsent letters to my father and to myself. These letters became a space to pour out my anger, my sorrow, and eventually, my gratitude. They allowed me to express what I could not say out loud, creating a symbolic release of the emotions I had carried for so long. Another transformative moment came during a guided meditation focused on forgiveness. Visualizing myself setting down the weight of my resentment and walking away from it, brought a sense of peace I had not felt in years.

As our childhood wounds are often carried into adulthood, we unconsciously repeat the patterns we learned from our parents. For me, these patterns manifested as a fear of vulnerability, a reluctance to trust and a tendency to push people away before they could abandon me. Although in the past, these behaviors were my way of protecting myself, they also kept me from forming deep and meaningful connections. Self-forgiveness allowed me to unlearn these patterns. It helped me to see that I was not defined by my past, that I had the power to break free from the cycle of pain that had been passed down through generations. By forgiving myself for the ways I had hurt others and allowed myself to be hurt, I was able to begin building healthier, more fulfilling relationships. In that space of forgiveness, I began learning how to set boundaries, to communicate my needs and to be vulnerable without fear of rejection.

It's important to recognize that forgiveness and closure don't always go hand in hand. Forgiveness is about emotional release whereas closure is about resolution and accepting that some relationships may never be fully healed. For me, closure came not from repairing my relationship with my father but from repairing the relationship I had with myself. With letting go of the expectation I had for him or us, I chose to focus on the man I wanted to become. I found closure in accepting the relationship for what it was, rather than what I wished it could be.

Self-compassion is another layer to forgiveness as they are deeply intertwined. To truly forgive, we must first be willing to extend compassion to ourselves—to recognize that we are human and that it is okay to make mistakes. For me, giving myself permission to feel the pain of my past without letting it consume me, was an act of self-care. It meant acknowledging the ways in which I had been hurt but also the ways in which I had inevitably hurt myself by holding onto that pain.

Deciding to forgive is about making a conscious choice every day to release the past, to let go of anger, and to embrace compassion. This practice has been essential part of my journey, not just in healing my relationship with my father but in all aspects of my life. It has allowed me to approach conflicts with empathy, and to see the humanity in others, even when their actions have caused pain.

For fathers and sons, the act of forgiveness can be a powerful tool in healing their bond. Even if full reconciliation is not possible, forgiveness can still be a path to peace as it allows both father and son to move forward without the weight of the past. Forgiving my father helped me see him as a human being navigating his own struggles. Forgiving myself allowed me to see that I was worthy of love, just as I was. Together, these acts of forgiveness have been the cornerstone of my healing journey.

The path to forgiveness and closure is not easy, but it is one of the most profound journeys you can take. It is a journey that leads not to perfection but to peace. It teaches you to embrace the imperfections of life, to find beauty in the brokenness, and to move forward with grace and compassion. This is the path I choose to carry forward—a life grounded in love, forgiveness, and healing.

EPILOGUE

AN INVITATION TO HEALING

The journey between fathers and sons is never straightforward. It is a dance of love, pain, misunderstanding, and the hope of reconciliation. This book is not just about repairing a bond—it's about the courage to face yourself, to confront patterns that no longer serve you, and to choose growth, even when the path forward feels uncertain. Healing is an act of bravery, a decision to reclaim your story and reshape your legacy.

Whether you're a father, a son, or someone carrying the weight of a fractured relationship, know this: you are not defined by what you lacked. You are defined by the strength it takes to choose love and forgiveness, for yourself and for others. The healing we undertake as individuals will create ripples that break cycles and creates healthier legacies. Our journey toward healing, understanding, compassion, and forgiveness becomes a gift—not only to ourselves but also to those who follow in our footsteps as the work we do on ourselves is not just for today; it's for tomorrow's relationships, tomorrow's families, and tomorrow's stories.

The process of healing is not without its challenges. It demands we confront old wounds, sit with uncomfortable truths, and relinquish the comfort of familiar patterns. But in doing so, it will also reveal the beauty of resilience—the power to transform pain into strength, and longing into love. Growth, in all its complexity, is both the hardest and most rewarding journey we can take. It teaches us to embrace our imperfections, honor our progress and trust in the process of becoming.

For me, this journey has been deeply personal and transformative. Writing this book has been my declaration to break cycles, to honor my boundaries, and to find peace even when full reconciliation isn't possible. In the process of releasing anger, practicing forgiveness, and embracing self-compassion, I've learned to forgive my father, not to absolve him but to free myself—from the burden of aiming for perfection and for holding onto the belief that I needed to be. These acts of forgiveness have been the cornerstone of my healing and the foundation for the relationships I nurture today.

As you move forward, let self-forgiveness guide you. Embrace your humanity, honor your progress, and allow yourself to be both imperfect and whole. The act of loving yourself as you are is perhaps the most powerful legacy you can leave. When you offer that same compassion to others, you create space for connection, understanding, and the possibility of healing—even in relationships that remain unresolved.

Remember, closure is not about forgetting or pretending everything is okay but instead, finding peace with what is. It's about accepting that some things may never be resolved and some relationships may never be fully healed. Closure is something we create for ourselves, a reclamation of power and peace that allows us to move forward without the shadow of the past looming over us. For me, closure came from repairing the relationship I have with myself, not the relationship I have with my father.

The story doesn't end here—it evolves with every step you take toward healing. Each conversation, choice, and moment of self-reflection adds a new chapter to your story. There is no definitive ending, only the ongoing promise of growth and connection. Let this book be a starting point, a companion, or a small light in your own journey.

Lean into your healing, but also share it. Speak openly, reflect deeply, and love courageously. Write your own story—not defined by the pain of the past but by the hope of what lies ahead. The legacy we build, whether as fathers, sons, or simply as individuals, begins in the choices we make today. This is your invitation: to heal, to grow, and to create a future rooted in compassion, understanding, and love. You are worth every moment of it.

thank you

&

happy healing

— axel

ACKNOWLEDGMENTS

What began as hours-long conversations with friends—about pain, love, childhood, relationships, and aspirations—became the foundation of this book. Those conversations revealed a deeper story, one rooted in healing and growth, and one that I felt compelled to share.

In no particular order, I want to extend my deepest gratitude to those friends who sat with me through those long and sometimes challenging talks. PF, EK, JW, TT, RD, JD, CD, MA —your friendship has been a lifeline, guiding me toward self-love, trust, resilience, and support. You've shown me the power of connection and encouraged me to embrace determination and appreciation on this path.

To Elisa, my mother: your generous heart, your courage, your strength, your infectious laugh, and your "no BS" attitude—along with your constant support—have inspired me in more ways than I can list here. Thank you for being the remarkable woman you are and for passing on that strength to me.

To Bianca, my incredible sister: thank you for being my rock. You've been there for me as a friend, a constant support, and someone who always speaks the truth with love. Your unwavering presence has been one of my greatest gifts, and I am endlessly grateful for your honesty, strength, and loyalty.

To Bryana, my therapist: thank you for your insight, patience, and belief in my potential. Your guidance has been invaluable in helping me confront my challenges and realize my capacity for growth.

You've empowered me to see my journey from a place of compassion and courage.

To my wonderful and beautiful partner… you have reshaped my understanding of love and partnership. You've supported my growth, stood by me through some of the best and hardest parts of healing, and shown me a love that is both accepting and inspiring. I am endlessly grateful for the blessing of you and the kindness, patience and understanding you bring to my life.

And finally, to everyone reading this book, or any of my work: thank you. By engaging with these words, you are a part of this journey—both mine and yours. Thank you for choosing to explore, to heal, and to grow. Your commitment to self-discovery fuels the spirit of this book and I am honored to share this path with you.

ABOUT THE AUTHOR

Axel Jordan is a visionary musician, celebrated author, master certified sound healer, and certified CBT & REBT coach practitioner dedicated to helping individuals unlock their fullest potential. With a personal journey rooted in healing and self-discovery, Axel specializes in guiding others through transformation by combining sound therapy, talk therapy, and holistic practices.

Born and raised in Brooklyn, NYC, Axel's diverse cultural and musical upbringing deeply influences his unique approach to emotional and mental well-being. In his first book, *SONS &*

SHADOWS: How Fathers Shape Their Sons' Future, Axel

delves into the profound dynamics of the father-son

relationship, offering readers heartfelt reflections and

practical tools for healing, growth, and self-discovery.

Axel's passion lies in helping others rebuild

self-worth and navigate life's challenges with

compassion and strength. His work as a sound healer,

specializing in celestial alchemy, and as a coach has

inspired countless individuals to embrace their own

transformative journeys.

When he's not writing, recording, or

working with clients, Axel leads sound bath healing

sessions and seminars that foster deep connections

between mind, body, and spirit. At home, he enjoys

time with his supportive partner and the animals they

foster, embodying the values of love and care he

advocates in his work.

also by Axel Jordan

365 Days Of Affirmations

HEALING (of) HEARTS

LOVE NOTES

Coming soon,

The Journey Back
Beyond Lust

www.AxelJordanBooks.com

Cover Design: Axel Jordan

ISBN: 979-8-89686-142-3

Library of Congress Control Number: 2024924251

ATTENTION: SCHOOL AND BUSINESSES

Any published works of Axel Jordan are available at quantity discounts with bulk purchase for educational, business, or sales promotional use.

For information, please contact sales department:
www.AxelJordanBooks.com